*S*PORTS GREAT

VINCE
CARTER

BASKETBALL

SPORTS GREAT CHARLES BARKLEY REVISED EDITION
0-7660-1004-X/ Macnow

SPORTS GREAT LARRY BIRD
0-89490-368-3/ Kavanagh

SPORTS GREAT MUGGSY BOGUES
0-89490-876-6/ Rekela

SPORTS GREAT KOBE BRYANT
0-7660-1264-6/ Macnow

SPORTS GREAT TIM DUNCAN
0-7660-1766-4/ Torres

SPORTS GREAT PATRICK EWING
0-89490-369-1/ Kavanagh

SPORTS GREAT KEVIN GARNETT
0-7660-1263-8/ Macnow

SPORTS GREAT ANFERNEE HARDAWAY
0-89490-758-1/ Rekela

SPORTS GREAT JUWAN HOWARD
0-7660-1065-1/ Savage

SPORTS GREAT MAGIC JOHNSON REVISED AND EXPANDED
0-89490-348-9/ Haskins

SPORTS GREAT MICHAEL JORDAN REVISED EDITION
0-89490-978-9/ Aaseng

SPORTS GREAT JASON KIDD
0-7660-1001-5/ Torres

SPORTS GREAT KARL MALONE
0-89490-599-6/ Savage

SPORTS GREAT REGGIE MILLER
0-89490-874-X/ Thornley

SPORTS GREAT ALONZO MOURNING
0-89490-875-8/ Fortunato

SPORTS GREAT DIKEMBE MUTOMBO
0-7660-1267-0/ Torres

SPORTS GREAT HAKEEM OLAJUWON REVISED EDITION
0-7660-1268-9/ Knapp

SPORTS GREAT SHAQUILLE O'NEAL REVISED EDITION
0-7660-1003-1/ Sullivan

SPORTS GREAT SCOTTIE PIPPEN
0-89490-755-7/ Bjarkman

SPORTS GREAT MITCH RICHMOND
0-7660-1070-8/ Grody

SPORTS GREAT DAVID ROBINSON REVISED EDITION
0-7660-1077-5/ Aaseng

SPORTS GREAT DENNIS RODMAN
0-89490-759-X/ Thornley

SPORTS GREAT JOHN STOCKTON
0-89490-598-8/ Aaseng

SPORTS GREAT ISIAH THOMAS
0-89490-374-8/ Knapp

SPORTS GREAT CHRIS WEBBER
0-7660-1069-4/ Macnow

SPORTS GREAT DOMINIQUE WILKINS
0-89490-754-9/ Bjarkman

For Other *Sports Great titles* call:
(800) 398-2504

VINCE CARTER

Jeff Savage

—SPORTS GREAT BOOKS—

Enslow Publishers, Inc.
40 Industrial Road   PO Box 38
Box 398   Aldershot
Berkeley Heights, NJ 07922   Hants GU12 6BP
USA   UK
http://www.enslow.com

Library of Congress Cataloging-in-Publication Data

Savage, Jeff, 1961-
    Sports great Vince Carter / Jeff Savage.
       p. cm. — (Sports great books)
    Includes index.
    Summary: Traces the basketball career of Vince Carter, former North
Carolina University basketball star and Toronto Raptor superstar known
for his ability as a slam-dunk artist.
    ISBN 0-7660-1767-2
    1. Carter, Vince—Juvenile literature. 2. Basketball players—United
States—Biography—Juvenile literature. [1. Carter, Vince. 2. Basketball
players. 3. African Americans—Biography.] I. Title. II. Series.
GV884.C39 S38   2002
796.323'092—dc21

                            2001003071

Printed in the United States of America

10 9 8 7 6 5 4 3

To Our Readers:
We have done our best to make sure all Internet addresses in this book were active and
appropriate when we went to press. However, the author and the publisher have no con-
trol over and assume no liability for the material available on those Internet sites or on
other Web sites they may link to. Any comments or suggestions can be sent by e-mail to
comments@enslow.com or to the address on the back cover.

Illustration Credits: NBA Photos/Andrew D. Bernstein, pp. 16, 21; NBA
Photos/Fernando Medina, pp. 8, 12; NBA Photos/Frank McGrath, p. 46; NBA
Photos/Glenn James, p. 48; NBA Photos/Nataniel S. Butler, pp. 10, 36, 38, 51;
NBA Photos/Ron Turenne, pp. 18, 41, 57, 59, 61; University of North
Carolina, pp. 25, 27, 29, 31.

Cover Illustration: NBA Photos/Frank McGrath

Contents

1 Slam Dunk! 7

2 Growing Up 14

3 Tar Heels 24

4 Rookie of the Year 34

5 Quest for the Playoffs 45

6 Becoming the Best 55

Career Statistics 63

Where to Write
and Internet Addresses 63

Index 64

Chapter 1

Slam Dunk!

Vince Carter stepped onto the court with a little-boy grin. The 16,000 fans at The Arena in Oakland moved to the edge of their seats. Carter was in the middle of putting on a show at the 2000 NBA.com Slam Dunk contest, and the crowd was not about to miss his next trick. Even the other National Basketball Association (NBA) superstars who were in town for the All-Star game the next day were lined up courtside to see Carter's aerial acrobatics. "Vince is a highlight reel," said Toronto Raptors teammate Tracy McGrady before the competition. "Everybody is going to be excited to see what he can do."

They had already seen Carter's first two dunks—a 360-degree spinning windmill one-hander, and a behind-the-back thunderslam. Both dunks received perfect scores of 50 from the courtside judges. The flying-dinosaur mascot on Carter's jersey representing the Raptors was the perfect fit for the young star known as Air Canada.

Carter's skywalking was no secret. Fans around the world recognized him on TV as the soaring six-foot six-inch guard with the shaved head and the handsome face. They had cast 1,911,973 votes for him for the All-Star game, easily the most of any player, and the second-highest total since fan balloting began many years earlier. Amid the presence of other superstars like Shaquille O'Neal,

Vince Carter put on a one-man show at the 2000 NBA.com Slam Dunk contest. Even his fellow NBA All-Stars had lined up to watch Carter fly.

Kobe Bryant, Tim Duncan, and Kevin Garnett, the buzz all week was about Carter. Now fans in California were seeing firsthand what kids in Toronto who wore Vince's No. 15 jersey had seen up close—the high-flying fireworks of Carter.

Carter prepared for his third dunk by positioning himself several steps from the basket. Meanwhile, McGrady stood near the top of the key with the basketball. This would be some sort of team dunk. At the signal, McGrady threw the ball on one high bounce toward the lane. Carter sprang from the floor like someone on a pogo stick, to catch the pass. He passed the ball between his legs, from front to back, then brought the ball up over his head. He was high in the air now, as if suspended from an invisible rope. All at once he snapped the ball into the net with a whipcrack. Then he floated softly back to the floor. "I wanted to come out with a bang," he said.

Fans burst from their seats. Players were on their feet and running like little children in all directions. Philadelphia 76ers star Allen Iverson raced up the tunnel shouting, "Vin-sanity, baby! I love it!" Even Carter's five dunk competitors cheered. Carter's face glowed as he skipped up to a courtside television camera and mouthed the words "It's over." It was a flamboyant gesture from a player whose greatest appeal to many is his humility. Carter's body may be in the air, but he keeps his head grounded. He has no tattoos, no earrings or other body piercings. He never brags. He tries to avoid the superstar hype that surrounds him. Carter was once asked whether his ego ever gets too big. He thought for a moment. "Well," he said, "sometimes, if I have a really good dunk in a game, I'll go home and watch it on the highlight shows."

All five judges awarded Carter 10s, for another perfect score of 50. He advanced easily to the final round, along with McGrady and Houston Rockets star Steve Francis.

Vince Carter's gravity-defying moves on the basketball court earned him the nickname "Air Canada."

Eliminated were Jerry Stackhouse of the Detroit Pistons, Larry Hughes of the Philadelphia 76ers, and Ricky Davis of the Charlotte Hornets. Carter was thrilled to reach the two-dunk final, and he could not help smiling and waving to his mother in the stands. "I know she's proud," he said.

McGrady and Francis each made one impressive dunk in the final round. McGrady received a score of 45 for performing a two-handed power dunk, and Francis earned a 48 with a reverse, back-to-the-basket, two-hand slam. But neither player had a chance on this night. This was Vince Carter's show. On his first dunk, Carter gripped the ball like a cantaloupe, got a running start, scissored his skinny legs through the air, and jammed the ball with his arm deep in the webbing of the net. He actually hung on the rim by the crook of his arm for a moment. The crowd roared again as the judges gave him straight 10s. "My favorite player," said Shaquille O'Neal. "Half man, half amazing."

Carter completed his amazing performance with a running dunk in which he launched himself from one step inside the free-throw line and soared forty-one inches— nearly three and a half feet—in a graceful glide to the rim, where he delivered a two-handed flush. He received three 10s and a pair of 9s for his final effort, to cap a nearly perfect evening. Hall of Famer George Gervin, one of the contest judges, said afterward that "the scoring system is not right for Vince Carter. You've got to be able to give more than a 10. He needed to be getting 15s or 20s on some of them."

Reporters surrounded Carter in the locker room afterward. "When I stepped on court," he said, "I didn't have any idea in the first round what I was going to do. The one between the legs, when Tracy bounced it, I made that up right before. By far the hardest one was the assist that Tracy bounced for me. Because you have to catch the ball

Despite all his accomplishments in the NBA, Vince Carter never brags. He always does his best to avoid the hype surrounding him.

and be able to put it between your legs, and at the same time still be able to make the dunk. That was my favorite."

As Carter spoke, players and league officials came over to shake his hand or give him a hug. Even former superstars Magic Johnson and Julius Erving stopped in to congratulate him. It was almost too much for Carter to comprehend. "It's unbelievable," he said. "I mean, it's unbelievable. It's hard for me to believe that I was just in the NBA dunk contest. I remember back in the days when my friends and I used to tape them and watch them, just watch them over and over again. I guess today is my day."

Chapter 2

Growing Up

Vincent Lamar Carter was born January 26, 1977, in Daytona Beach, Florida. He was raised by his mother, Michelle Carter-Robinson, and his stepfather, Harry Robinson, in a blue-gray two-story house a few minutes from the beach. His mother and stepfather worked hard as schoolteachers and were great role models for their two sons. Carter has one brother, Chris, who is three years younger.

Vince played basketball on his driveway with a hoop that stood over eleven feet in the air. (A regulation rim stands ten feet.) Maybe that is why Vince always aspired to reach so high. It was on this driveway that Vince learned the basic fundamentals and joy of basketball. "I started playing with my first basketball when I was two," said Carter, "and I joined my first team when I was seven." Vince enjoyed playing such other sports as football, soccer, and volleyball. At age eight, he joined the Daytona Beach Centipedes of the Pop Warner football league. The following year, he played for the Port Orange Hawks. He liked having the ball in his hands, and he was a skilled athlete, so he played quarterback. But basketball was always his first love.

Vince's two best friends growing up were Joe Giddens and Cory Brown. "Vince was just a really nice kid," said

Joe. "He shared everything he had. If he had candy or food, he'd give me and Cory some. If he had an extra basketball, he'd just let me have it for free. He was just that way. His mom and stepdad raised him to be a good person. That's why you don't see the tattoos or the earrings or the attitude from Vince. He would never be that way. He wouldn't know how. He just liked to have fun and share. The three of us always hung out together. Cory and I were Vince's right hand and left hand."

By sixth grade, Vince had grown to be five feet eight inches tall. That summer he dunked for the first time. In the nearby town of Ormond, Joe's mother, Joanne Giddens, would open the doors to the Nova Gym to Vince and Joe on weekends and at night so they could play basketball against high school players. Vince honed his skills against the taller boys and grew in confidence. He had other interests, like playing the saxophone and other instruments because of his stepfather's influence as the music teacher at Mainland High School. He was an excellent student at South Daytona Beach Elementary School, where his favorite subject was reading. But he dreamed of basketball. He was determined to be a pro.

At Campbell Junior High School, Vince became the first seventh grader to ever play on the varsity team. A year later the family moved north to Ormond, where they had built a two-story brick house. It featured a basketball hoop in the driveway, of course. Vince attended Ormond Middle School in eighth grade. At a community basketball clinic that year, he was spotted by Dick Toth, the varsity coach at Mainland High. Coach Toth returned to school astounded. "I've just seen the starting point guard for Mainland for the next four years," he told the other coaches. "This kid is amazing. He can do anything!"

At Mainland High, Vince starred in basketball, track, and volleyball. His mother attended nearly every event.

Vince Carter grew up playing basketball in his driveway with a hoop that stood over eleven-feet high—more than a foot higher than a regulation NBA rim.

"She would be at everything," said Vince. "Basketball games, basketball camps, band, volleyball, anything. She would be there." At basketball games, Vince's mother watched her son play point guard for the varsity as a freshman. "Florida is football country," said Assistant Coach Charles Brinkerhoff. "When I first heard about Vince, I wondered how much basketball coaching he'd had. I wondered if he could handle playing with the varsity team. Sometimes if you put a kid on the floor with the big boys too soon, he gets frustrated. But Coach Toth insisted that Vince play on the varsity and be the starting point guard. And then I saw why."

Vince was six feet one inch tall and could sky. He could have played any position, even center. "He had incredible talent," said Coach Brinkerhoff. "And he was an avid learner. He was a good listener and very receptive to coaching. You knew right away that he wanted to get better, that he wanted to be great."

Mainland High struggled to a 14–15 record in Vince's first year. Losing was frustrating. "He would get impatient real easy," his mother said. "Sometimes I'd have to tell him to relax, calm down, and go to a movie or something." Vince relaxed best by playing the saxophone. He still plays it today. He even played the alto and tenor sax in the school's marching band. "Guys still hear that and make fun of me," Vince says now. "But trying different things and doing what I like is more important than being popular."

Coach Brinkerhoff took over as head basketball coach when Vince was a sophomore. Joe Giddens, who was a year younger than Vince, enrolled at Mainland that year. "Please, Coach Brink," Vince pleaded, "let Joe be on the floor with me. We play so good together." The coach agreed, and the fortunes of the Buccaneers soared. Cory Brown served as the team's manager, standing behind the bench to give the players Gatorade or towels, and now the

By the time he reached the seventh grade, Carter was playing for the varsity basketball team.

three buddies were together again. The Bucs rolled to a 20–5 regular season record to reach the district playoffs. They beat Deltona High, 68–48, in the first round, before suffering a heartbreaking loss in the next round. The Bucs led Deland High by six points late in the game, when the scoreboard clock failed. It took technicians fifteen minutes to repair the clock. Deland High had a chance to regroup. Deland forged a tie in the final minute. With time running out, Mainland freshman T. T. Toliver missed a shot. Then Deland's point guard hit a driving scoop shot at the buzzer to win it, 56–54. Vince and his teammates were devastated. "He hated to lose, but he didn't sulk," said Coach Brinkerhoff. "Some kids get angry and lose their composure. Not Vince. When he lost, which wasn't often, he would get with Giddens and Toliver and his other buddies and talk about it. He would be quiet and reflective. He would learn from it." Vince averaged 18.7 points and nearly eight rebounds a game as a sophomore. He could not wait to prove he could do more.

In the classroom, Vince was a model student. He always sat in the front row. He was prepared each day to study, and he always turned in his work on time. He liked reading even more now, and he enjoyed writing poetry. He even helped write the school's homecoming song—a pop number to a hip-hop beat. "He was such a happy student," said his friend Joe. "You could just look up in the hallway and there he would be, the tallest kid, wearing glasses and a smile on his face, and carrying his book bag."

In the summer, Vince tuned up his game by playing with a traveling team from New Jersey called Paterson Catholic. Future NBA player Tim Thomas also was on that team. Vince's nickname with Paterson was Sunshine, because he was from Florida—the Sunshine State. He returned to Mainland for his junior season as a star. He averaged more than 25 points and 11 rebounds a game and shot 60 percent from the field inside the three-point arc, 37 percent from three-point range. Most impressive were his dunks. He had become an acrobat now, sending them down in creative ways. He amassed 55 dunks as a junior, and the students at Mainland gave him a new nickname— UFO! Playing various positions on the floor now, Vince led the Bucs to a 24–1 record and into the playoffs with as good a chance as anyone to win the state title. He did this despite the pressure of knowing he was under the watchful eye of college coaches and scouts. The coaches were not allowed to talk to him, but they contacted him by mail, and he knew they were in the stands. The schools interested in him read like a top 25 poll. Among them were Duke, North Carolina, Villanova, Kansas, Kentucky, Michigan, and Florida.

With Vince leading the way, Mainland rolled through the playoffs, beating six teams in a row, including Pensacola High, 67–61, in the regional final, after trailing by ten points in the second half. Mainland had not won a state title in fifty-five years, and after a 72–53 triumph over Fletcher High of Jacksonville in the quarterfinals, the Bucs were two wins away. But in the semifinal round, they fell behind Boyd-Anderson High by ten points. They rallied to get within three late, but fell short, 66–61. Vince was disappointed with the loss, yet proud of his team's 30–2 final record. "We can go farther next year—and we will," he vowed.

Vince spent part of his summer as a member of 1995 USA Basketball Junior team that played in the World Championships in Mannheim, Germany. His sensational dunking was now creating an international stir. Back in school for his senior year, he was the drum major for the marching band, and he was even offered a college scholarship from nearby Bethune-Cookman to be the school's drum

Vince Carter's role models were his parents, who were both teachers. In the classroom, Vince always sat in the front row and was a model student.

major. Vince was honored, but he preferred a scholarship in basketball.

By now, coaches were meeting with him at his school and his house. Dean Smith and Bill Guthridge of North Carolina visited him. So did coaches Tommy Amaker, Matt Dougherty, Phil Ford, and even Mike Krzyzewski of Duke. The name Vince Carter became popular nationally in the high school ranks. Over 10,000 fans went to the Kiel Center in St. Louis, Missouri, to see his team beat national power Collinsville of Illinois, 52–35, in the prestigious KMOX Shootout holiday tournament. Back in Daytona Beach, the Ocean Center was crammed with 6,100 fans to watch the Bucs pound Seabreeze High, 96–47, as Vince led the way with 19 points and six dunks.

At his home gym, affectionately known as Buccaneer Paradise, Vince celebrated his eighteenth birthday in an 80–55 win over Lake Mary High of Orlando, with a school record 17 blocks to go with 26 points, 16 rebounds, and 8 assists. His season scoring average dipped from his junior year to 20 points a game, but as Coach Brinkerhoff said, "It showed his unselfishness. Vince knew that to win the state championship he had to get more people involved. He had to be a total team player. He was, and it paid off."

Mainland cruised through its first six games of the play-offs to reach the state semifinals for the second year in a row. At the Leon County Civic Center, they built a 15-point lead over mighty Miami Senior High with five minutes to go when Vince fouled out of the game. The Bucs held on for dear life as Miami stormed back and closed to within two. But point guard T. T. Toliver sank six straight free throws in the final two minutes to finish with 20 points, and Joe Giddens added 15 to save the day in a 70–67 victory. Two nights later, in the state 6A title game, Vince's triple-double of 22 points, 16 rebounds, and 10 blocks carried the Bucs to a convincing 62–45 win over

Dillard High of Ft. Lauderdale. It was the perfect finish to an exciting high school experience.

After Vince Carter joined the Raptors, he wrote a letter to his school that read: "I just want to thank Mainland High for giving me my start at basketball. Playing professional ball was my lifelong dream, and it has come true with the solid foundation Mainland gave me. Thank you. Vince Carter. Class of '95."

Chapter 3

Tar Heels

Carolina Blue. Those two words represent the deep tradition of men's basketball at the University of North Carolina. Vince Carter was recruited by most of the nation's top college programs. In the end, he was left with one choice—Carolina Blue. "I was recruited by schools like Duke, Florida State, and Florida," he said, "but I picked UNC because it's a good school, and, most importantly, I felt comfortable from the beginning with UNC."

Dean Smith was already a coaching legend when Carter arrived in the fall of 1995. Assistant Bill Guthridge, who would later take over for Smith, was another coaching wizard. Together they stressed the importance of academics. This pleased Carter's mother, Michelle, who wanted her son to get his college degree. Deep down, Michelle knew that Carter had the talent to make it to the NBA. Players were allowed to leave college early to join the pros, and Michelle knew that if things went well for her son on the court, he could skip out early. She wanted him to get a solid education before doing so, and she asked him to promise her that no matter what, he would somehow get his college degree. She even had him sign an agreement.

Carter lived on campus in a dormitory. One of his roommates was another prized recruit named Antawn Jamison. The two freshmen became fast friends. Among

North Carolina Head Coach Dean Smith was already a basketball legend when Vince Carter arrived at the school in the fall of 1995.

their favorite times was playing pickup ball with the great Carolina grad Michael Jordan, who came to Chapel Hill often. When things began slowly for Carter, it was Jordan who told him to keep his head up. Carter listened closely to his coaches, and halfway through his freshman year, he began to play more. Coach Smith did not like playing freshman. He had written his only newspaper article ever thirteen years earlier for *The New York Times* and called it "Why Freshmen Should Not Play." Smith believed that freshmen should sit and learn. But Carter and two other freshmen on the team—Jamison and Ademola Okulaja— were simply too good to keep on the bench. By the time the Atlantic Coast Conference (ACC) games began, Carter was a starter at guard, and Jamison and Okulaja were starting forwards. They called themselves "The Three Musketeers." In the ACC opener against North Carolina State before a sold-out crowd of 21,572 at the Dean Dome, Carter scored a season-high 18 points to lead the Tar Heels to a 96–72 victory. He scored in double figures in ten games, including 14 points against eighth-ranked Wake Forest in which he had five second-half baskets, including a spectacular reverse layup that cut Wake Forest's lead to two. He capped the game with a soaring alley-oop slam as the Tar Heels won, 65–59. Carolina reached the NCAA Tournament, which comprises a field of sixty-four teams, but the Heels bowed out early in a second-round loss to Texas Tech.

Carter worked hard in the spring and summer to improve his game in all areas. When the 1996–97 season began, Coach Smith called Carter the best defensive player on the team. He had the quickness to guard smaller opponents and the strength to defend under the basket. He was versatile on offense as well, with an explosive burst to the basket and a smooth outside shot. North Carolina's standard plan of attack is to spread the ball around so that the

When Carter's college career got off to a slow start, he received encouragement from the great Michael Jordan. Carter continued to work hard and his playing time increased as a result.

defense cannot key on a single player. Carter still managed to score in double figures in twenty-five of the team's thirty-five games, including five games with 20 points or more. In the NCAA Tournament, the Tar Heels reached the Sweet 16 by defeating Fairfield and Colorado. In the round of 16, the Heels were locked neck-and-neck with California late in the game when Carter took over. With the score tied at 48, he took an alley-oop pass and slammed it down for the lead. After a Cal miss, he dribbled down-court, pulled up from behind the arc, and buried a three. Cal never recovered. Carolina's 63–57 victory propelled it into the Elite 8. At the East Regional Final against Louisville, a sold-out crowd of over 30,000 fans at the Carrier Dome in Syracuse, New York, watched Carter score 13 points in the first half to push the Tar Heels to a 21-point advantage. The game seemed out of reach. But the Cardinals of Louisville fought back to close within three. That's when Carter made the biggest basket of Carolina's season. He took the ball down the left baseline past three defenders and hit a floating runner. The momentum changed, and the Tar Heels roared to a 97–74 triumph.

Carter saved his best for last. In the Final Four semifinal game against Arizona, in front of 47,028 fans at the Hoosier Dome in Indianapolis, Carter nailed six of eight shots for 16 points in the first half on his way to collecting 21 points, 6 rebounds, and 4 steals. But Arizona roared back in the second half to win, 66–58, and end Carolina's season.

Carter went right back to work that summer, practicing his footwork and shooting touch, hoping to take his game to the next level. One day he got a telephone call from Tracy McGrady. Carter knew the kid from pickup games on campus. Carter was even nice enough to let McGrady store his gear in Carter's locker. McGrady had just graduated from high school and was skipping college to go straight to the NBA. He would play in cold Toronto for the upstart Raptors. McGrady was very excited on the phone. He had just learned at a family reunion that he and Carter were related! It turned out that McGrady's and Carter's grandmothers were cousins. "I started freakin' out," said McGrady. "I couldn't wait to tell Vince!" After talking on the phone, the young men decided to keep in touch.

North Carolina began the 1997–98 season with the same lineup as the year before. The difference was, Coach Smith had retired. Bill Guthridge took over, and the Tar Heels did not miss a beat. They were ranked fourth in the country in the preseason poll, and after five weeks they moved into the No. 1 spot. With Okulaja, Jamison, and center Mahktar Ndiaye up front, guards Shammond Williams and Ed Cota distributing the ball, and Carter

Carter and fellow freshmen Antawn Jamison and Ademola Okulaja became known as "The Three Musketeers" at UNC.

playing everywhere on the floor, the Heels were nearly impossible to stop. Jamison would be named the National Player of the Year. For his part, Carter would become known nationally as a dunking machine. He even kept a list of opposing players that he dunked on. Reporters loved talking to Carter about his dunks. "What's your favorite dunk you ever made?" they asked. "Either the one from Villanova or Wake Forest," he would say. "What is your favorite type of dunk?" Carter would turn to Jamison. "Antawn, what's my favorite dunk?" Antawn would reply, "It's gotta be the windmill, Vince." Carter would smile and say, "A one-handed windmill."

Plenty of opponents saw Carter's windmill dunk up close. Carolina rolled through the season winning its first seventeen games before the streak was snapped in overtime at Maryland. The Tar Heels closed the regular season with a 27–3 record and their second straight Atlantic Coast Conference title. Carter averaged 15.6 points and 5 rebounds a game, and an impressive shooting percentage of .590. The Heels drubbed Navy in the first round of the NCAA Tournament but needed overtime, and Carter's 24 points, to slip past UNC-Charlotte, 93–83, in the second round. In the East Regional semifinal, Carter and Jamison scored 20 points each to beat Michigan State, 73–58, and two days later the Tar Heels advanced to the Final Four for the second straight year with a 75–64 win over Connecticut. But at the Alamodome in San Antonio, Texas, the Heels fell into a deep hole with poor shooting, to fall sixteen points behind Utah in the first half. Carter did all he could to dig his team out by hitting ten of sixteen shots to finish with a game-high 21 points. But the rest of the team shot just 32 percent for the game, and North Carolina's season ended with a 66–59 loss.

Carter was honored after the season as a First-Team All-Atlantic Coast Conference and Second-Team All-America

After the 1997–98 season, Carter decided to leave school early and take his high-flying moves to the NBA.

choice. Individual awards were fine, but the only selection Carter was interested in now was the NBA draft. He had decided to forgo his senior year in college to enter the NBA. Most draft experts said Carter had the best pure talent of any player available and predicted he would be among the top six picks. The NBA determines draft order by a lottery drawing. The lottery is weighted in favor of the teams with the worst records. This meant Carter would likely be picked by a losing team. On the bright side, this would give Carter a better chance to play more for his pro team. Who knew? Maybe he could even break into the starting lineup.

Carter and his family sat among dozens of other premier college players and their families at New Jersey's Continental Arena for the NBA draft. They listened nervously as the first three players were chosen. The Toronto Raptors had the fourth selection. They drafted Carter's college teammate, Antawn Jamison. The Golden State Warriors were up next. They did not hesitate. They quickly selected Carter. Now it was official: Vince Carter's lifelong dream to be a pro basketball player had come true.

Then NBA commissioner David Stern stepped to the lectern to announce a trade. The Raptors were swapping draft choices with the Warriors. Jamison was going to the Warriors, and Carter was headed to Toronto to play for the Raptors. He hadn't even dribbled an NBA basketball yet, and already he was being traded! Carter was overjoyed. He would be joining his cousin Tracy McGrady with the Raptors. Also, the Raptors had wise veteran forward Charles Oakley on their team. Oakley and Michael Jordan were good friends. Jordan called Oakley and asked him to please look out for the rookie Carter.

Carter's family was thrilled. But as far as his mother was concerned, there was still some unfinished business. Back home in Daytona Beach, Michelle approached Carter her son with a piece of paper in her hand. It was the agreement that he had signed three years earlier, promising her that he would get his college degree. "My mother took that paper out of a drawer and waved it at me," Carter said. Then Michelle put the paper back in the drawer. Nothing was said. Nothing needed to be.

Chapter 4

Rookie of the Year

Toronto is a hockey town. The rich history of the National Hockey League's Maple Leafs has deep roots that stretch for decades. Could basketball survive in a hockey town? In 1995, the NBA decided to try. They created the Toronto Raptors, along with another expansion team, the Vancouver Grizzlies, in hopes that Canadians were ready for the sport. The Raptors were only three years old when Carter joined them. As expected, the team had suffered difficult growing pains. In fact, the Raptors were so bad the year before, finishing with a 16–66 record, that after the season's last game, general manager Glen Grunwald stood at center court and apologized to the fans. Grunwald asked Toronto fans not to give up. He promised that the team would be better.

Carter was eager to help, but he had to wait. The 1998–99 season was delayed because of a players' strike. After three months of bickering over how to divide billions of dollars, the players and owners settled their dispute, and the season finally began. Carter started with a bang. In his NBA debut on February 5, 1999, in front of nearly 18,000 fans at the Fleet Center in Boston, Massachusetts, he poured in 16 points and grabbed 3 rebounds to help the

Raptors to a season-opening 103–92 victory over the Celtics. Four nights later, at the team's home opener at the newly built Air Canada Centre, Carter led his team in scoring with 22 points in a loss to the Milwaukee Bucks. Carter was making a statement that he would be an immediate impact player. "As far as skill level goes," said Miami Heat Head Coach Pat Riley, "the sky is the limit for that guy."

Opposing teams tried to attack Carter, as they do all rookies. But Carter's veteran teammates taught him to protect himself. Charles Oakley showed him how to read double-teams and how to defend pick-and-rolls. Kevin Willis taught him how to study opponents' strengths and weaknesses. Doug Christie explained to him how to play hard through a grueling season. Dee Brown helped him handle the new demands he faced off the court. "Any time I had a question," said Carter, "at games, locker room, practice, at home, all I had to do was ask and there would be someone with an answer."

One thing his teammates did not have to teach Carter was how to dunk. He showed he could play among the tall trees by sending down one rim-rattling jam after another. There was his baseline double-pump reverse jam against the Indiana Pacers. And his body-bump and dunk on Dikembe Mutombo, the 1998 Defensive Player of the Year. Players marveled at Carter's talent. "I've never seen anyone in the NBA jump as high as Vince," said Seattle Supersonics forward Vin Baker. The NBA even installed the Vince Carter NBA Jam Cam on its Web site. But Carter could do more than dunk. As Jamal Mashburn of the Miami Heat said, "He's more than just a jumper. The real basketball fan, the purist, knows Carter is fundamentally sound. He can play!" Opponents scurried to try to find a way to defend Carter, especially when he got loose in the open floor. As Pacers scout Al Menendez said, "Once he builds up momentum to the basket, he's going to do

After a players' strike delayed the start of his rookie season, Vince Carter scored 16 points and grabbed 3 rebounds in his first NBA game as the Toronto Raptors defeated the Boston Celtics.

something spectacular. You have to try to force him away from the basket. Or hope he trips along the way." Just ten games into the 1999 season, basketball fans in Toronto were already uttering an unfamiliar word: playoffs. The arrival of Carter had changed the mood. Carter refused to accept any credit. "Me? I'm just playing off youth and athleticism. I'm still learning the NBA game," he said. "I can put a little IQ to it now, but really, the four old guys, including Doug Christie, they're the backbone."

Meanwhile, Carter was still adjusting to life in the north. After all, he was a thousand miles from home in Daytona Beach, in a city where it's often fifty degrees colder in wintertime. "It's not Florida, but you learn to adjust," he said. "And the people of Canada have accepted me. It's cool." Carter had moved into a luxury apartment on the banks of Lake Ontario in downtown Toronto. McGrady and two other Raptors lived in the same apartment complex. He drove a black Navigator each day to the arena for practice. Sometimes for fun he went to an arcade on Yonge Street near his home. With his collar turned up and his cap pulled low, as if he were in disguise, he would play *Doom II* and other games. Mostly, though, he usually hung out in his apartment, playing on his PlayStation or listening to music from his enormous CD collection. He had electronic gadgets throughout the condo, and four remote controls on his coffee table to operate them. "I don't know my way around as much as I would like," he said. "I don't go out much. I know enough to survive. I know where the grocery store is and where the arena is. I just really stay home, listen to music, play video games and surf the Internet."

Meanwhile, out in California, Carter's Tar Heel buddy Jamison was struggling with the Golden State Warriors. Jamison was said to be too small to play power forward and too large to play small forward, and he was trying to find

Life in Canada was an adjustment for Vince Carter. It was a thousand miles away from his hometown in Florida and much colder, especially in the wintertime.

his role with the team. He averaged less than 10 points and barely played twenty minutes a game. Jamison had always been "The Man", and now he was struggling to compete. Carter tried to keep his friend's spirits up with weekly phone calls. "I tried to help him stay positive. I knew what he was capable of," said Carter. Jamison appreciated the encouraging words. "I knew Vince was trying not to make me feel bad," he said, "because things were going so much better for him than they were for me." It would take Jamison two more years to emerge as the Warriors' top offensive threat. In the meantime, Carter spent hours a day on the telephone with Jamison and other friends, running up monthly tabs of $1,500 or more. His most frequent calls were to Daytona Beach. His family would gather in front of the television to watch the Raptors, and after every game Vince would call home. "I talk to my parents a lot," he said. "We are really close. My mother critiques my game. She always tells me to stay focused in everything I do."

Carter developed a tight bond with Tracy McGrady. They spent as much time in each other's apartment as their own. On the team bus, Carter would sit in the front of the bus, McGrady in the back, and they would talk to each other on their cell phones. "They say they're cousins," said guard Dee Brown. "But Siamese twins is more like it."

In mid-March, Carter carried his team to four straight wins by leading them in scoring with 20, 28, 26, and 23 points. In one game at Detroit, he stole victory from the Pistons by scoring six points in the final minute on three drives to his left for dunks. With the clock winding down in a tie game, he forced a bad pass, then hit the winning shot in a 103–101 triumph. For his efforts, he became the first Raptor ever to be named NBA Player of the Week. Carter was finally willing to accept some credit. "I didn't plan for it to be this way," he admitted. "My goal was to fit in, gradually work my way to being an impact player. My whole scheme fell through from Day One."

At the Air Canada Centre on April Fool's Day, Carter scored his team's last six points again, on a twenty-foot fadeaway over Reggie Miller, a burst past three defenders for a dunk, and an offensive tip-in, to give the Raptors an 88–87 win over the Pacers. Two nights later, against the Washington Wizards, he saved an 87–85 victory by forcing Mitch Richmond to put up an air ball at the buzzer. Two nights after that, he led the team past the Philadelphia 76ers for its ninth straight home victory. "I'm not sure what happened," said Carter, "but all of a sudden, we believe." The Raptors were 18–14 and on the verge of reaching the playoffs for the first time ever. Two days later against the Miami Heat, Carter made an amazing highlight-reel dunk with a feint to his left, a burst past Jamal Mashburn, and a ferocious slam over defensive stalwart Alonzo Mourning. But the Raptors lost the game, their first of six straight losses. Carter did what he could to halt the slide, teaming with McGrady in one game to score 50 of the team's 99 points. But it was not enough to dig Toronto out of a funk that cost the team a trip to the playoffs.

Carter closed the season in style with a breakaway 360-degree reverse jam in a win over the Cleveland Cavaliers. There was optimism for the first time in Toronto for its basketball team. "The excitement here is unbelievable," said veteran Antonio Davis, who spent most of his career in Indiana. "The Pacers won games, but I don't think we were exciting to watch. With Carter and swingman Tracy McGrady getting up and down the court and dunking, this will be a whole different look." Or, as Carter said, "We're not considered a cupcake anymore. Winning has given us confidence, so look out!"

Better yet, look out for Vince Carter! The six-foot six-inch guard proved he was a complete player by leading the

Carter is congratulated by teammate Mark Jackson after drawing a foul. In his first year in the NBA, Carter was the only rookie to lead his team in scoring.

Raptors—and all NBA rookies—in points scored and blocked shots. In fact, he was the only rookie in the league to lead his team in scoring. He was a runaway choice for the 1999 NBA Rookie of the Year.

Carter spent his first off-season summer in Chapel Hill, where he focused on three things: devoting time to children, working toward his college degree, and improving his game. He met often with kids at sports camps, as on the day he drove to Charlotte to visit the J. C. Smith basketball camp. He talked about the importance of studying, and then played some pickup ball with the group. One sixteen-year-old boy bodied up on Carter and paid for it when Carter dunked in his face. The boy shouted that he would always cherish the moment. Another kid gushed, "Your dunks are crucial, Vince. Just crucial!"

On campus at Chapel Hill, Carter earned nine credits toward his degree by taking classes in computers, communications, and African-American studies. In the gym, he worked mainly on his defense and his outside shooting. NBA legend Larry Bird had observed during the season that, "if Vince works on his shooting a little bit, he could be unstoppable." So, that's just what Carter did, taking more than a thousand shots a day. "Some days," he said, "I shot 1,500."

The 1999–2000 season started on time. It could not have come soon enough for Carter. "Last season was great," he said, "but it feels like ancient history. I'm ready to keep showing what I can do. When I say ready, I mean, I'm ready now."

Toronto featured a starting lineup of front-liners Charles Oakley, Antonio Davis, and Tracy McGrady, point guard Doug Christie, and, of course, Carter. The Raptors were ready from the start. They won three of their first four games before traveling to Detroit to face the Pistons. "Who am I guarding?" Carter asked Coach Butch Carter.

"Grant Hill," the coach replied. Carter grinned. He was glad to guard the other team's best player. Carter seized the opportunity with 22 points and 11 rebounds while holding Hill to 6-for-22 shooting in Toronto's convincing 123–106 win.

Six days later, the teams met again in Toronto, and Hill had a chance for revenge. He did not get it. Carter shut him down again, this time on 4-of-15 shooting. Meanwhile, Carter scored 22, to lead his team to an 89–85 win. "Coming from Carolina," Carter said afterward, "you weren't going to play much unless you played defense." All that Hill, a Duke graduate, could say was, "You should have gone to Duke."

The Raptors traveled to Los Angeles for the season's tenth game. They had never beaten the Lakers on the road—until now. Carter scored a career-high 34 points and grabbed 13 rebounds to carry his team to a 111–102 triumph. It was a statement game. It showed the rest of the league that the Raptors, indeed, were no longer a cupcake. Two weeks later, against the defending champion San Antonio Spurs, Carter stepped up again, pouring in 39 points, a new career high, in a 98–92 victory. "We won on our way to becoming a good basketball team," he said. "We got a chance to see where we stand."

Carter's outside shooting was often the difference in games. He had shot less than 29 percent behind the three-point arc as a rookie (the league average was 33 percent), but this year he was shooting over 40 percent from three-point range. The hard work over the summer was paying off. Carter was fast becoming popular with fans around the country who saw him as a happy, backslapping, easygoing player who looked like he was having fun on the court. There were even whispers of Carter, with his dunking acrobatics, becoming the next Michael Jordan. In fact, the similarities were eerie. Both players attended the

University of North Carolina. Both left for the NBA after their junior year. Both won the Rookie of the Year award. Both were six feet six inches tall with shaved heads and bright smiles. And both could jump to the moon. Carter dismissed the comparison. "Everybody today has flashes of playing like Mike sometime. He changed the way the game is played," said Carter. "It's a great compliment. I'm honored by the comparison. But I'm my own person. I am who I am. I want to establish my own identity. I don't want to be the next Michael Jordan. I want to be the first Vince Carter."

Chapter 5

Quest for the Playoffs

The nightly sports highlight shows could not get enough of Vince Carter. They featured his spectacular dunks nearly every time he played. They showed him knifing through the defense and—wham!—sending down a rim-rattler. They showed him getting ahead of the defense in the open floor and—whoosh!—gliding through the air while contorting his body in some crazy way. Players around the league admitted to hurrying home after games to watch the highlights to see Carter's next wild move. "He's probably the most exciting individual in basketball right now," said All-Star Shawn Kemp. "He's a joy to watch." *ESPN Magazine* even named Carter its athlete for the new millennium. Former great Magic Johnson, another wizard with the ball, said Carter was in position to take over the game. "We're still waiting for someone to take up where Michael [Jordan] left off," said Johnson. "It's actually just waiting to be grabbed. Vince Carter is emerging as someone who could be the one. Maybe it's Kobe [Bryant]. Whoever it is has to win championships."

Carter seemed the perfect candidate for the league's new poster boy. His cheery attitude carried him even further. "He's as good as advertised," said guard Dee Brown.

"And the best thing is he's down to earth. He's got a personality to go with it. He's not arrogant. He's just a nice kid from Florida." Why, then, was Carter about to be ignored in such a shocking way?

The 2000 Olympic Games were approaching. The nine-person USA Basketball selection committee gathered to assemble a team. In a 6–3 vote, it chose Milwaukee's Ray Allen over Carter. The decision stunned many NBA experts. Pacers coach Isiah Thomas, a former Olympian, said, "Clearly, when you look at Vince Carter, if he's not the best two-guard playing right now . . . well, I don't know what the people were looking at." Sacramento Kings general manager Jerry Reynolds added, "Ray is really good, but it's hard to put Ray Allen ahead of Vince Carter. Vince

As the 1999–2000 season began, Vince Carter was quickly being recognized as a star NBA player. His amazing plays were being shown on sports highlight programs nearly every night he played.

is about flash, youth, and excitement." Raptors General Manager Glen Grunwald simply said, "Vince deserves to be on the team. He's one of the best players in the world right now."

Carter was devastated. Playing in the Olympics was a lifelong dream. He tried to put it out of his mind. When reporters asked him about the snub, he shrugged and pretended he was over it. "I didn't make it," he said. "I'll have another chance in four years. It would have been a great opportunity, but it gives me a chance to grow and get better. Hopefully, in four years, there will be no doubt." Deep down, Carter was hurt and angry.

Soon after, the final results for fan balloting for the 2000 NBA All-Star Game were released. Carter was the leading vote-getter. Such news was the perfect medicine to lift his spirits. He had received nearly 2 million votes from fans throughout North America. He would start at guard for the Eastern Conference in the game at The Arena in Oakland, California. Carter and teammate Tracy McGrady and several team officials flew out Thursday afternoon for All-Star Weekend. Carter and McGrady would compete in Saturday's slam dunk contest, and Carter would play in Sunday's game. As Raptors officials dined on shrimp cocktail, prime rib, and champagne on the flight west, Carter sat back and munched on a twenty-piece pack of Chicken McNuggets. The next day he went to a local elementary school to meet with students and talk about the joy of reading.

Saturday was the dunk competition. Carter took flight with imagination and grace to soar past his competition. Afterward, he was asked by reporters whether he still kept a list of players he dunks on, as he did in college. Carter said he did not keep a list, but that he simply remembered. "Zo? Yeah, I got him," he said of Miami Heat center Alonzo Mourning. "[Dikembe] Mutombo? Got him

Carter hugs the Toronto Raptors' mascot. Nineteen of the Raptors' last twenty-eight games of the 1999–2000 season were sellouts. Basketball was gaining a lot of fans in Canada thanks to Carter.

twice," he said of Atlanta's seven-foot center. "Got the big dude in Indiana, [Rik] Smits. Got Dale Davis, too. Haven't gotten [Patrick] Ewing yet." Then Carter paused and smiled. "We play them on Tuesday."

In the All-Star game the next day, Carter wore a microphone so fans watching on TV could hear him on the court. Among the first sounds they heard was Carter celebrating as he ran up the court after catching a lob pass from Allen Iverson and performing a dramatic double-clutch reverse sidewinder dunk. Carter played twenty-eight minutes and made six of eleven shots for 12 points, and also collected 2 rebounds and 2 assists as the East fell to the West, 137–126. "It might never happen again, you never know," Carter humbly told reporters afterward. "So I was just living it up, enjoying the scenery, playing with someone like Allen Iverson and on down the line." For many of the All-Stars, Carter was all the scenery they needed. Asked what he enjoyed most about the weekend, co-MVP Shaquille O'Neal said, "Watching Vince, of course. I've never seen anyone do stuff like that."

Two nights after the All-Star game, Patrick Ewing's New York Knicks were at the Air Canada Centre. Eight minutes into the game, Carter slammed over Ewing. Then he took his game outside to nail baseline jumpers and three-pointers in a fifteen-point first-quarter blitz on his way to scoring 29 in a 91–70 rout of the Knicks. The Raptors improved their record to 27–24 and were a real threat to make the playoffs for the first time in the franchise's five-year history.

Until now, one criticism of Carter's game was that he was too generous. He would pass up shots and give the ball up instead. His coach and teammates always implored him to shoot more. But Carter said, "Every time I step out on the court, I'm always looking to give the ball up, to get assists. I don't mind scoring the points that we need to win, but I don't mind passing the ball either."

Carter's attitude was about to change. In a nationally televised game against Phoenix he poured in a career-high 51 points in a 103–102 win. Three nights later at Boston he drilled a game-winning three-pointer, as he was falling out of bounds in the right corner at the buzzer, to beat the Celtics, 96–94. Four days later he scored 10 straight points down the stretch, to beat the Vancouver Grizzlies, 92–88. Three nights later in Los Angeles he hit another buzzer-beater jumper, to nip the Clippers, 95–94. He was playing with a different attitude now. He smiled less and scowled more. "There's no time for me to smile," he said. Asked whether he was mad about being left off the Olympic team, he said, "Yeah, it helped me step up. I said to myself, 'OK, you just have to show the world what you can do night in and night out.'"

The torrid pace continued. He scored 35 points to win at Portland. He scored 23 against Golden State, including the final eleven, after spraining his ankle. He hit a three-pointer with twenty-nine seconds left against Houston, and then drove the baseline past Shandon Anderson and over Hakeem Olajuwon for a game-winning slam with one second to go. "Once he got off, I don't think anybody could have blocked it," said Anderson. "He only took one dribble and jumped. There was no time to recover. He was pointing, pointing, then bam!"

Bam! Carter had taken his game to a higher level. "In the playoffs there won't be any time for fun," he said. "It's time to get serious. That mentality has been taught to me by Oakley and the older guys, and I understand what it takes to win." That is what the Raptors were doing— winning. The victory over the Rockets was their eleventh in twelve games. They stood at 39–26 now, a sure bet to make the playoffs. Many people insisted that Carter had become the best player in the NBA. "I'm not the best player in the league," he responded. "Not at all. Not yet. I have to just continue to get better. I figure I will be one of the best players in the league when I can help my team win consistently. Not sometimes. Not six in a row. But maybe 17, 18 in a row." But Carter had many believers, such as Philadelphia coach Larry Brown, who said, "Vince is playing at another level. The Raptors are winning all the close games. That young fellow is doing things that have to give the team so much confidence, knowing that if they're in the ball game, Vince will figure out a way to win. I love the way Vince plays and how he conducts himself."

Carter's confidence and fierce drive paid off in more ways than victories. It was learned that Phoenix Suns

Vince Carter is defended by the Los Angeles Lakers' Kobe Bryant. Carter finished the 1999–2000 season fourth in scoring with his 25.7 points per game average.

forward Tom Gugliotta would miss the rest of the season after undergoing knee surgery. Gugliotta would also be unable to play in the Olympics. The committee needed a replacement. The choice was easy. "It's an honor," said Carter, after being told he had made the Olympic team. "I hope I can represent the USA well. It's a great opportunity to be in the Olympics, and I'm looking forward to playing with the guys and winning a gold medal. That's the most important thing." The Games would begin in September. Now it was time to finish the season.

As the Raptors fought for playoff position down the stretch, a new sense of excitement enveloped Toronto. Nineteen of the team's last twenty-eight home games were sellouts. That was an accomplishment in Canada, where hockey rules. In Vancouver, for instance, only one game was a sellout all year—the game against the Raptors. "That's because of Carter," said Jay Triano, Canada's Olympic team coach. "Shareef Abdur-Rahim, Michael Dickerson, and Mike Bibby are stars in Vancouver, but Carter is an international star playing in Canada, exposing even more kids to the sport."

Toronto's final regular-season home game was a thrilling come-from-behind 85–84 win over the Chicago Bulls. Afterward, music blared, and hundreds of purple balloons floated down from the rafters as thousands of fans cheered and watched the season's highlights on the big screen overhead. The veteran players waved to the crowd and ran off to the locker room. Not Carter. He and Tracy McGrady stayed on the court, laughing and batting the balloons in the air. They wanted to enjoy the party. And why not? For Carter it was an unforgettable second season. He finished fourth in the NBA in scoring at 25.7 points per game. He shot over 40 percent from three-point range. He was named to the All-NBA third team.

Next came the playoffs. The Raptors were matched in

the first round against the New York Knicks. In the regular season, Carter was a nemesis against the Knicks, averaging 33 points a game while leading the Raptors to three wins in four games. Ten days earlier, Carter dominated the Knicks with 34 points in an 86–71 thumping.

The playoffs were a different story. The Knicks double-teamed Carter throughout the series, even sending two defenders out to half-court to guard him as he brought the ball up. Latrell Sprewell held him to 30 percent shooting in the three-game sweep. Game 1 was the worst of it. On Easter Sunday at New York's Madison Square Garden, Carter missed his first twelve shots and made just three of twenty all day. "I was overexcited," he said. "I wasn't my normal self."

The Raptors still had a chance to steal the game when Carter nailed a three-pointer with 2:25 left to tie it, 81–81. The score was tied again, 85–85, with forty-two seconds left, when Larry Johnson drilled a three for the Knicks. Carter sank one free throw to cut the margin to 88–86, but it was not enough as the Raptors lost, 92–88. Carter was devastated. He was unusually quiet on the plane ride home as his teammates tried to cheer him up. "We're not going to let him put his head down for one bad shooting night," said veteran Antonio Davis. "He's done too much for this team."

But Carter could not shake out of his funk. Once in Toronto, he drove his black Navigator home to his condo and crawled into bed. He awoke the next morning before his alarm clock went off, and he felt refreshed. He was ready to put his awful performance behind him. "I was up early, and that's not like me," he said. "I was just sitting in bed saying, 'All right, it's a new day.'" He drove to practice eager to prepare for Game 2.

Back in New York, two nights later, Carter was back to normal, hitting soft jumpers and throwing down monster dunks. He racked up 27 points to put the Raptors in position to even the series at a game apiece. But the Knicks hung tough, and when Sprewell hit a short jumper with eight seconds left, it gave New York its first lead since the opening moments of the game. The Raptors had time for one last shot. Carter was the likely choice to take it. The Knicks would be double-teaming him. Could he shake free to get another chance? Yes. He caught a pass and left his feet from twenty-five feet out with three seconds left. But in midair, he passed to teammate Dee Brown for an open three-pointer from the wing. Brown missed. The buzzer sounded. The Raptors lost again. "I was feeling confident, but looking out of the corner of my eye, Dee was wide open," Carter explained. "He's a great shooter, and you take your chances." Brown's shot was straight on, but long. "Vince gave me a good pass," said Brown. "I just didn't hit the shot."

The Raptors had to win three straight games to advance. It was too much to ask. In Toronto for Game 3, the Knicks led by two points, 80–78, and had the ball with half a minute left. The Raptors needed a stop. With the shot clock winding down, Larry Johnson let fly with a three-pointer from straightaway. It banked in! "Did you call glass?" Carter asked. "No!" Johnson replied. Suddenly, New York had a five-point lead with twenty-four seconds left. "That's a shot you make in H-O-R-S-E," said Carter afterward. "He makes that shot at a crucial point in the game, it's tough to come back from."

The Raptors did not come back. They lost, 87–80, and their season was over. Carter removed his sneakers and tossed them to the crowd. He trudged into the locker room shoeless and winless. "Reality hit real quick," he said. "You say to yourself you're not going to come back and play basketball. The season is over. Now I've got to go home and watch my cousins and nephews."

Chapter 6

Becoming the Best

While his Toronto Raptors teammates spent the summer relaxing, Vince Carter had a date in the Land Down Under. He was scheduled to go with Team USA to Sydney, Australia, for the 2000 Olympic Games. First, though, Carter needed to spend some time in Chapel Hill. "I made a promise that I would go back to school to finish my education," he said, "and that's what I intend to do." Ten weeks later, Carter received his college degree from the University of North Carolina. His agreement with his mother had been fulfilled.

In Australia, Carter and his basketball teammates were surprised at the harsh treatment they received. Fans booed them as if they were evil giants. Their team was composed of mostly NBA superstars, and so it was far more talented than teams from any other country. But that was not the players' fault. They could not help being great. Still, the U. S. team was one everyone loved to hate. Some American players complained about the booing. Some even got angry. But Carter said the booing "doesn't bother me at all." As Carter explained, "My mom always told me, 'You could be an angel and walk a straight line and someone's going to have a problem with you.' So I don't care what people think about me." Carter just wanted to concentrate on basketball. And his teammates were glad he did.

Carter made such fantastic plays that the fans momentarily forgot they were rooting against the Americans and actually let out great gasps and cheers. In the first half of a 93–61 rout of Italy, Kevin Garnett threw an alley oop that appeared much too high for Carter to reach. But Carter leaped high to swipe the pass off the glass and slam it home. The crowd went berserk. In a game against France, Carter intercepted a pass and took off for the basket with seven-foot two-inch center Frederic Weis in his way. Carter jumped from the foul line, scissor-kicked his legs to climb still higher, and launched his body right over Weis. He flew completely over the mammoth center and threw down a ferocious dunk. It might have been the most spectacular basketball play ever in the history of the Olympic Games. "I don't have time to worry about who's there," Carter said. "I just put the ball in the hole." Said teammate Jason Kidd: "Michael Jordan hasn't done that, nobody's done that!" Team USA coach Rudy Tomjanovich said, "The only time I've ever seen a play like that is when I jumped over my four-year-old son on one of those Nerf ball baskets." Even Weis himself joked, "I was thinking to take a charge, but then he jumped over me."

The U. S. team cruised to the medal round, where it met Lithuania in the semifinals. That's when the fun stopped. Lithuania fought back from a twelve-point halftime deficit to tie the game, 80–80, with forty-four seconds left. The heavily favored Americans were on the brink of an embarrassing loss. Ramunes Siskauskas made a free throw to give Lithuania a one-point lead. Kidd answered with a layup to steal the lead back for the United States. Then Carter stole the ball and was fouled. He missed both free throws. Fortunately for Team USA, Antonio McDyess grabbed the rebound off the second miss and put the ball

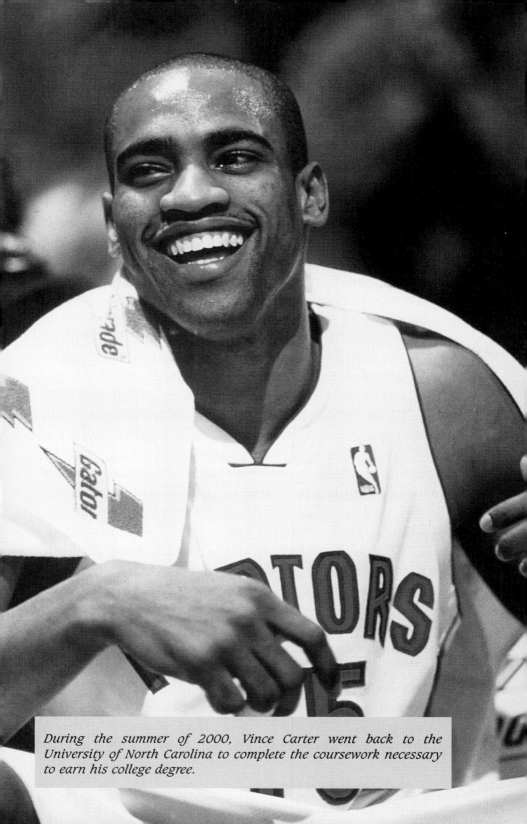

During the summer of 2000, Vince Carter went back to the University of North Carolina to complete the coursework necessary to earn his college degree.

back in for a three-point lead. A layup by Lithuania cut the lead to one again. Kidd made a free throw with nine seconds left to stretch it to two. Lithuania took the last shot—a three-pointer—to try to win it. No good! Team USA won, 85–83, and averted disaster. "We didn't lose," said Carter, who led the team with 18 points. "I don't care what the world thinks. Look at the scoreboard."

In the gold-medal game, the U. S. team was not about to let France come so close. When the French team crept to within four points with 4:24 left, Kevin Garnett hit a short jumper, Alonzo Mourning added two free throws, and Carter punctuated it with a double-pump, reverse jam. Team USA won, 85–75, to capture Olympic gold.

Carter was thrilled to return home with a gold medal. At the same time, he was eager to play NBA ball again. Unfortunately, he would have to do so without Tracy McGrady, who left to join the Orlando Magic as a free agent. "The fans have to understand it's a business," said McGrady, "and I have to do what's best for me."

Carter was disappointed to see McGrady go, but he believed the Raptors could win without him. And he was right. Toronto lost its first three games before getting on track with four straight wins in pursuit of the playoffs. As the season entered 2001, Carter led the NBA in scoring, thanks to such pinball scores as 48 points against the Milwaukee Bucks, 45 against the Indiana Pacers, 40 against the Charlotte Hornets, and 39 against the Philadelphia 76ers—all Raptors victories. "There's no answer for stopping him," said Dallas Mavericks coach Don Nelson. "He jumps over the rim. He shoots the heck out of it, with range. He can dribble it. He can pass it. He can rebound. He can defend. What else is there?"

All around the Toronto area, thousands of kids were wearing Carter's No. 15 jersey. At the Raptors' official souvenir shop downtown, it was the only jersey for sale, available in some thirty styles and colors. "That's the only one we need," said the shop manager. Carter's likeness appeared on billboards across Canada in candy advertisements and in a national television commercial he went one-on-one in a basketball contest against a velociraptor dinosaur.

"Vince is very goal oriented," said his mother, Michelle. "The students at a Toronto high school that he visited recently asked about his goals, and he said he had to set new ones because he made the Olympic team, the All-Star team, and the playoffs." But as far as Carter tries to go, he always remembers where he came from. He remains true to his friends. "When I need someone to talk to, he's there," says lifelong pal Joe Giddens. "And when he needs

Vince Carter stretches during warm-ups before a game. At the 2000 Olympics in Sydney, Australia, Carter helped the United States team earn a gold medal in men's basketball.

someone, I'm there, too. There's a lot of pressure on him, you know, with all the fame and the autographs, and when it gets tough, we'll just talk about an old subject, like high school, or a time when he missed a dunk. You know, just keep it light. We'll play hoops or with the PlayStation. We'll go to the mall where the first place he always goes is the music store. Whatever the newest music is, he's gotta have it. The next stop is always for a chicken sandwich. And, of course, he takes me to games. He flies me up to Toronto. Next month I'll be hanging with him at All-Star Weekend in Washington, D.C. He's such a great friend. I'm just glad he didn't forget about me."

Carter will forever remain faithful to his roots. When he was given $10,000 for winning the 1999–2000 NBA Sportsmanship Award, he gave the money to the Mainland High School basketball team and marching band. Vince Carter has also established his own charitable foundation for disadvantaged children, called Embassy of Hope. In addition to providing hundreds of thousands of dollars to children in need, the foundation is planning to build a home for neglected and abused children, to be called Vince's Village. "It's something Vince really wants to do," said Embassy of Hope secretary Ann Smith. "He wants to give children who need help a good opportunity like he had."

Carter's biggest mission of all is to encourage children to read. Recently he funded a program called Read With The Pros, which is a newspaper insert for students that provides reading activities using sports as the theme. In the insert is an open "Letter from Vince" that says: "I really can't imagine a world without reading. You can go any-where you want to go, be anyone you want to be, and do anything you want to do. Wow, what fun!" Carter also says in the letter, "Remember that it doesn't matter how many things you are good at doing. Being able to read and knowing

Off the court, Carter's biggest mission is to help encourage kids to read. He funded his own program called Read With The Pros, and is a spokesman for the NBA's Reading Is Fundamental (RIF) program.

what you have read will give you the foundation and vehicle to reach your goals."

Carter also is the star for the NBA's Reading Is Fundamental (RIF) program. A national TV commercial shows Carter sitting under a tree, where he hears some birds chirping. He looks up into the tree but does not see the birds. Then he realizes that the birds are in the book that he is holding.

Vince Carter's primary job with the NBA is playing basketball, of course. He is known worldwide as the most flamboyant dunk artist in the game, but those who understand the game know he is much more. He has a feathery shooting touch, makes pinpoint passes, plays stifling defense, and is the ultimate team player. And he is getting better all the time. "Dunkers come and go," Carter says. "You can go down to the playground and find a bunch of guys who can do fancy dunks. The great players excel at all aspects of the game. That's what I want to be. I'm willing to learn, and I'm willing to wait my turn. I have to keep playing hard, keep learning, keep getting better, and one day I could be the best player in the NBA." Many say he already is the best.

Career Statistics

College

SEASON	TEAM	GP	FG%	REB	PTS	PPG
1995–1996	North Carolina	31	.492	119	232	7.5
1996–1997	North Carolina	34	.525	152	443	13.0
1997–1998	North Carolina	38	.591	195	592	15.6
Totals		103	.547	466	1,267	12.3

NBA

SEASON	TEAM	GP	FG%	REB	AST	STL	BLK	PTS	PPG
1998–1999	Toronto	50	.450	283	149	55	77	913	18.3
1999–2000	Toronto	82	.465	476	322	110	92	2,107	25.7
2000–2001	Toronto	75	.460	416	291	114	82	2,070	27.6
Totals		207	.460	1,175	762	279	251	5,090	24.6

GP=Games Played   **REB**=Rebounds   **BLK**=Blocks
FG%=Field Goal   **AST**=Assists   **PTS**_Points
Percentage   **STL**=Steals   **PPG**=Points Per Game

Where to Write Vince Carter:

Mr. Vince Carter
c/o Toronto Raptors
40 Bay Street, Suite 400
Toronto, Ontario 5MJ 2

On the Internet at:

http://www.nba.com/playerfile/vince_carter/index.html
http://www.nba.com/raptors

Index

B

Bird, Larry, 42
Brinkerhoff, Charles, 17, 22
Brown, Cory, 14, 17
Brown, Dee, 35, 39, 45
Brown, Larry, 51

C

Campbell Junior High School, 15
Carter-Robinson, Michelle
(mother), 14, 24, 59
Christie, Doug, 35

D

Davis, Antonio, 40
Daytona Beach, FL, 14

E

Embassy of Hope, 60
Ewing, Patrick, 49

G

Gervin, George, 11
Giddens, Joe, 14
Golden State Warriors, 32, 37
Grunwald, Glen, 34, 47
Guthridge, Bill, 29

H

Hill, Grant, 43

I

Indiana Pacers, 40
Iverson, Allen, 9, 49

J

Jamison, Antawn, 24, 26, 29, 30, 32,
37–39
Jordan, Michael, 26, 32, 43

K

Kemp, Shawn, 45
Kidd, Jason, 56

M

Magic Johnson, 45
Mainland High School, 15, 60
Mashburn, Jamal, 35
McGrady, Tracy, 7, 28–29, 39, 58
Menendez, Al, 35, 37
Mutombo, Dikembe, 35

N

NBA draft, 32
NBA Slam Dunk contest (2000),
7–13
Nelson, Don, 58
New York Knicks, 53

O

Oakley, Charles, 32, 35
Okulaja, Ademola, 26, 29
Olympic Games (2000), 46, 47, 52,
55–58
O'Neal, Shaquille, 11, 49

R

Reynolds, Jerry, 46
Riley, Pat, 35
Robinson, Harry, 14

S

Smith, Dean, 24, 26

T

Tar Heels, 26–31
Team USA, 55–58
Thomas, Isiah, 46
Tomjanovich, Rudy, 56
Toth, Dick, 15, 17
Triano, Jay, 52

U

University of North Carolina
(UNC), 24, 55

W

Willis, Kevin, 35